English Warm-ups

By

DEBORAH WHITE BROADWATER

COPYRIGHT © 2002 Mark Twain Media, Inc.

ISBN 1-58037-208-2

Printing No. CD-1554

Mark Twain Media, Inc., Publishers
Distributed by Carson-Dellosa Publishing Company, Inc.

Table of Contents

Introduction to the Teacher

It is important for students continually to work at improving their language arts and reading skills. This can be done with regular classroom instruction but should be reinforced on a regular basis.

This book is intended to offer the teacher and parent short warm-up activities to help the student practice the skills that are taught in the classroom. There are six mini-activities on each page of this book that can be used at the beginning of class to help students focus for the day on language arts and reading. The activities use language arts skills, such as grammar and sentence combining, as well as prompts to help students begin short writing pieces. Reading activities, such as main idea, fact or opinion, and analogies, are also included. In addition, there are pages practicing dictionary skills and spelling.

Each page may be copied and cut apart, so that the individual sections can be used as warm-up activities for each day of the week. Or the teacher may give each student the entire page to complete so he or she can keep it in a three-ring binder to use as a resource. Students may need to use their own paper to complete some of the activities, especially the story leads. The teacher could also make a transparency of the page, and the activities could be completed as whole-class activities, either in order or randomly.

Name: _____ Date: _____

English Warm-ups: Story Leads

Name/Date: _____
STORY LEADS 1

What items would you need if you were stranded on a desert island?

_____
_____
_____
_____

Name/Date: _____
STORY LEADS 2

Tell about your favorite vacation spot.

_____
_____
_____
_____
_____

Name/Date: _____
STORY LEADS 3

If you could be an animal, what would you be? Why?

_____
_____
_____
_____

Name/Date: _____
STORY LEADS 4

If you could teach a new subject at school, what would it be, and what would you include?

_____
_____
_____
_____

Name/Date: _____
STORY LEADS 5

Describe someone in the room.

_____
_____
_____
_____

Name/Date: _____
STORY LEADS 6

If a wet dog came running into the room right now, what would happen?

_____
_____
_____
_____
_____

Name: _____ Date: _____

English Warm-ups: Story Leads

Name/Date: _____

STORY LEADS 7

List all the words that come to mind when you think of snow.

_____
_____
_____
_____
_____

Name/Date: _____

STORY LEADS 8

Describe your face.

_____
_____
_____
_____
_____

Name/Date: _____

STORY LEADS 9

What kind of career would you like to have, and what do you need to be successful?

_____
_____
_____
_____
_____

Name/Date: _____

STORY LEADS 10

Write about a favorite character in a book.

_____
_____
_____
_____
_____

Name/Date: _____

STORY LEADS 11

If you received a letter from your favorite sports or movie star, what do you think it would say?

_____
_____
_____
_____

Name/Date: _____

STORY LEADS 12

Give instructions for making a peanut butter and jelly sandwich.

_____
_____
_____
_____

Name: _____ Date: _____

English Warm-ups: Story Leads

Name/Date: _____

STORY LEADS 13

Where would you like to spend your vacation and why?

_____
_____
_____
_____

Name/Date: _____

STORY LEADS 14

If there are people living on other planets, what are they called, and what do they look like?

_____
_____
_____
_____

Name/Date: _____

STORY LEADS 15

Describe the car of the future.

_____
_____
_____
_____

Name/Date: _____

STORY LEADS 16

List words that come to mind when you hear the word *rain*.

_____
_____
_____
_____

Name/Date: _____

STORY LEADS 17

What career would you choose and why?

_____
_____
_____

Name/Date: _____

STORY LEADS 18

If a genie could grant you one wish, what would it be and why?

_____
_____
_____

Name: _____ Date: _____

English Warm-ups: Story Leads

Name/Date: _____

STORY LEADS 19

What do you think your life will be like twenty years from now?

_____
_____
_____
_____
_____

Name/Date: _____

STORY LEADS 20

List words that come to mind when you hear the word *beach*.

_____
_____
_____
_____
_____

Name/Date: _____

STORY LEADS 21

What animal would make the best pet and why?

_____
_____
_____
_____
_____

Name/Date: _____

STORY LEADS 22

What would you do if you won a million dollars?

_____
_____
_____
_____
_____

Name/Date: _____

STORY LEADS 23

Describe your favorite flavor of ice cream without using the name of the flavor.

_____
_____
_____
_____
_____

Name/Date: _____

STORY LEADS 24

Make a list of words to describe a rabbit.

_____
_____
_____
_____
_____

Name: _____ Date: _____

English Warm-ups: Story Leads

Name/Date: _____

STORY LEADS 25

What additional sport do you think should be in the Winter Olympics?

_____
_____
_____
_____
_____

Name/Date: _____

STORY LEADS 26

Make a list of all the things you can think of that are blue.

_____
_____
_____
_____
_____

Name/Date: _____

STORY LEADS 27

How would you like to celebrate your birthday?

_____
_____
_____
_____
_____

Name/Date: _____

STORY LEADS 28

What would you tell someone new to your school about the school lunches?

_____
_____
_____
_____
_____

Name/Date: _____

STORY LEADS 29

If you were an animal trainer, what would you teach an elephant to do?

_____
_____
_____
_____

Name/Date: _____

STORY LEADS 30

Find something in the classroom and look at it carefully. Describe it without telling what it is.

_____
_____
_____
_____

Name: _____ Date: _____

English Warm-ups: Story Leads

STORY LEADS 31

If you were to invent a candy, what would it look like and taste like?

_____
_____
_____
_____
_____

STORY LEADS 32

Write the instructions to tell someone how to build a snowman.

_____
_____
_____
_____
_____

STORY LEADS 33

Who is your favorite author, and why do you like him or her?

_____
_____
_____
_____
_____

STORY LEADS 34

Describe your favorite breakfast.

_____
_____
_____
_____
_____

STORY LEADS 35

What are the three most important things to know if you are going to get a pet?

_____
_____
_____
_____
_____

STORY LEADS 36

Write the lead for a scary story. Make sure it is an "attention grabber."

_____
_____
_____
_____
_____

Name: _____ Date: _____

English Warm-ups: Story Leads

Name/Date: _____

STORY LEADS 37

Describe a radio or TV commercial that you like.

_____

_____

_____

_____

Name/Date: _____

STORY LEADS 38

I once saw the most amazing thing. It was ...

_____

_____

_____

_____

Name/Date: _____

STORY LEADS 39

Describe a good place to study and do your homework.

_____

_____

_____

_____

_____

Name/Date: _____

STORY LEADS 40

What is one thing you can do to make your school a better place?

_____

_____

_____

_____

_____

Name/Date: _____

STORY LEADS 41

Who is your favorite actor or actress and why?

_____

_____

_____

_____

Name/Date: _____

STORY LEADS 42

If this were your last day on Earth, what would you have for your last meal?

_____

_____

_____

_____

Name: _____ Date: _____

English Warm-ups: Story Leads

Name/Date: _____
STORY LEADS 43

What would be a good exercise
to help you stay healthy?

_____
_____
_____
_____

Name/Date: _____
STORY LEADS 44

Should students wear uniforms to school?
Give one good reason to support your answer.

_____
_____
_____
_____

Name/Date: _____
STORY LEADS 45

I'll never forget the time I ...

_____
_____
_____
_____

Name/Date: _____
STORY LEADS 46

What are some important things
to know about taking care of a
pet?

_____
_____
_____
_____

Name/Date: _____
STORY LEADS 47

What should you do when the fire
alarm rings?

_____
_____
_____
_____

Name/Date: _____
STORY LEADS 48

If you were the principal of your
school, what is the first rule you
would change and why?

New Rules

_____
_____
_____
_____

Name: _____ Date: _____

English Warm-ups: Grammar/Usage Skills

Name/Date: _____

GRAMMAR/USAGE 1

Add two adjectives and a noun to the following sentence.

Ben ran.

_____

_____

_____

Name/Date: _____

GRAMMAR/USAGE 2

Write three declarative sentences using five or more words in each.

_____

_____

_____

_____

_____

Name/Date: _____

GRAMMAR/USAGE 3

Write the plural of *child, ox,* and *mouse.*

_____

_____

_____

Name/Date: _____

GRAMMAR/USAGE 4

Draw an arrow from the subject to the verb in each sentence.

Jeff carried the ball to the field.

How many fish are in the bowl?

Name/Date: _____

GRAMMAR/USAGE 5

Correct the following sentence, and write it on the lines below.

I was late for school but I weren't marked tardy.

_____

_____

_____

Name/Date: _____

GRAMMAR/USAGE 6

Write a proper noun for each of the following words.

friend _____

pet _____

book _____

country _____

language _____

music group _____

Name: _____   Date: _____

English Warm-ups: Grammar/Usage Skills

Name/Date: _____

GRAMMAR/USAGE 7

Correct the following sentence.

babe ruth held the home run record for many years it was broke by hank aaron

_____

_____

_____

Name/Date: _____

GRAMMAR/USAGE 8

Correct the following sentence.

they maid their playhouse out of boxes there mother gave them.

_____

_____

_____

Name/Date: _____

GRAMMAR/USAGE 9

What are five adverbs to complete this sentence? Ruth runs ...

_____

_____

_____

Name/Date: _____

GRAMMAR/USAGE 10

Write five adjectives to describe water.

_____

_____

_____

Name/Date: _____

GRAMMAR/USAGE 11

Write the possessive of each of the following nouns: men, sisters, pennies, bananas

_____

_____

_____

_____

Name/Date: _____

GRAMMAR/USAGE 12

List eight nouns that are in your classroom.

_____

_____

_____

_____

Name: _____ Date: _____

English Warm-ups: Grammar/Usage Skills

Name/Date: _____
GRAMMAR/USAGE 13

Write six contractions.

_____
_____
_____
_____
_____

Name/Date: _____
GRAMMAR/USAGE 14

Correct the following sentence.

Puppies are born with there eyes closed, and it stays near the Mother Dog.

_____
_____
_____

Name/Date: _____
GRAMMAR/USAGE 15

Write three compound words using the word *mountain*.

_____
_____
_____
_____

Name/Date: _____
GRAMMAR/USAGE 16

Write a sentence using *its*.

_____
_____

Write a sentence using *it's*.

_____
_____

Name/Date: _____
GRAMMAR/USAGE 17

Correct the following sentence.

I would like too take spanish next year.

_____
_____
_____
_____

Name/Date: _____
GRAMMAR/USAGE 18

Complete the sentence by adding the subject.

_____ ran to school.

Now add two adjectives.

_____
_____

Name: _____ Date: _____

English Warm-ups: Grammar/Usage Skills

Name/Date: _____

GRAMMAR/USAGE 19

Correct the following sentence.

Our sci. teacher Mr. Langenbach show us how to do experiments.

_____

_____

_____

Name/Date: _____

GRAMMAR/USAGE 20

Choose *good* or *well* to complete the following sentences. Explain your choice.

Jamal didn't feel _____ after the trip.

I think that is a _____ book.

Name/Date: _____

GRAMMAR/USAGE 21

Write four adverbs to complete this sentence.

The cat stretched _____.

_____

_____

_____

Name/Date: _____

GRAMMAR/USAGE 22

List four contractions that don't end with *n't*.

_____

_____

_____

_____

Name/Date: _____

GRAMMAR/USAGE 23

Correct the following sentence.

Did you know that sum birds cant fly

_____

_____

_____

_____

Name/Date: _____

GRAMMAR/USAGE 24

Use the word *chair* in a sentence as a noun.

Use the word *chair* in a sentence as a verb.

_____

_____

_____

_____

Name: _____ Date: _____

English Warm-ups: Grammar/Usage Skills

Name/Date: _____

GRAMMAR/USAGE 25

Write four words that are written the same whether singular or plural.

_____

_____

_____

_____

Name/Date: _____

GRAMMAR/USAGE 26

Correct the following sentence.

A full-grown hummingbird ways only a few oz.

_____

_____

_____

Name/Date: _____

GRAMMAR/USAGE 27

Write two interrogative sentences that you might hear at school.

_____

_____

_____

_____

Name/Date: _____

GRAMMAR/USAGE 28

Many adverbs end in *-ly*. Think of four adverbs that don't end in *-ly*.

_____

_____

_____

_____

Name/Date: _____

GRAMMAR/USAGE 29

Correct the following sentence.

Using it's pause, the cat knocked the ball across the floor.

_____

_____

_____

Name/Date: _____

GRAMMAR/USAGE 30

Complete the following sentence with three adjectives.

Boys rode their bikes.

_____

_____

_____

Name: _____ Date: _____

English Warm-ups: Grammar/Usage Skills

Name/Date: _____

GRAMMAR/USAGE 31

Write a list of adjectives to describe the weather today.

_____

_____

_____

_____

Name/Date: _____

GRAMMAR/USAGE 32

List the pronouns that can be used as subjects. Choose two, and write a sentence for each on your own paper.

_____

_____

_____

_____

Name/Date: _____

GRAMMAR/USAGE 33

Write three imperative sentences.

_____

_____

_____

_____

Name/Date: _____

GRAMMAR/USAGE 34

Correct the following sentence.

don't stack the books to high they will fall over and hurt someone.

_____

_____

_____

Name/Date: _____

GRAMMAR/USAGE 35

Correct the following sentence.

first put on soxs and than put on shoos

_____

_____

_____

_____

Name/Date: _____

GRAMMAR/USAGE 36

List four nouns that are always plural.

_____

_____

_____

_____

Name: _____ Date: _____

English Warm-ups: Grammar/Usage Skills

Name/Date: _____

GRAMMAR/USAGE 37

Change these sentences to de-clarative.

Are you going to the movies?
Did Jason eat the cake?
How many books are on the table?

_____

_____

_____

Name/Date: _____

GRAMMAR/USAGE 38

Correct the following sentence.

woodrow wilson began the league of nations but the us never joined

_____

_____

_____

Name/Date: _____

GRAMMAR/USAGE 39

Write two sentences using *lay*.

_____

_____

Write two sentences using *lie*.

_____

_____

Name/Date: _____

GRAMMAR/USAGE 40

Write the past and past participle tenses of the following verbs.

swim _____

play _____

run _____

Name/Date: _____

GRAMMAR/USAGE 41

Write an antonym for each of the following words.

warm _____

quick _____

forget _____

fiction _____

shiny _____

midnight _____

Name/Date: _____

GRAMMAR/USAGE 42

Correct the following sentence.

Yes I think the the answer to question 1 should be mr washington

_____

_____

_____

Name: _____ Date: _____

English Warm-ups: Grammar/Usage Skills

Name/Date: _____

GRAMMAR/USAGE 43

Add three adjectives
and a pronoun to the
following sentence.

The dog slept on the blanket.

_____

_____

_____

Name/Date: _____

GRAMMAR/USAGE 44

Correct the following sentence.

the explorers who had traveled to mexico took
back gold and silver to there country.

_____

_____

_____

Name/Date: _____

GRAMMAR/USAGE 45

Some words change to plural by changing *f*
to *v* and then adding *es*. Write four examples
of this.

_____

_____

_____

_____

Name/Date: _____

GRAMMAR/USAGE 46

Write the abbreviation for each of
the following words.

Mister _____   doctor_____

street _____   January _____

Professor_____   hour _____

quart _____   avenue _____

Name/Date: _____

GRAMMAR/USAGE 47

Underline the subject once and the verb twice.

Stephen ran to the grocery
store.

Where is Stephanie?

Name/Date: _____

GRAMMAR/USAGE 48

Adverbs tell how, when, where, and how
many. Write a sentence that uses adverbs in
all four ways.

_____

_____

_____

_____

Name: _____ Date: _____

English Warm-ups: Dictionary Skills

Name/Date: _____

DICTIONARY 1

Number the words below, putting them in alphabetical order.

_____ enzyme   _____ balloon

_____ special   _____ doughnut

_____ carpet   _____ triple

Name/Date: _____

DICTIONARY 2

Say each dictionary pronunciation to yourself. Write the word. Check the dictionary to see if you are correct.

pē kän ´ _____

spăt _____

bēch _____

Name/Date: _____

DICTIONARY 3

Divide these words into syllables.

unusual _____

distance _____

important _____

Name/Date: _____

DICTIONARY 4

Circle the words that are between these two guide words on the dictionary page.

grant/grass

grasp   grape   guilty

grave   graph

Name/Date: _____

DICTIONARY 5

Circle the words that come before these guide words on the dictionary page.

bead/beautiful

baker   benefit   bask

beauty

Name/Date: _____

DICTIONARY 6

Using a dictionary, write the dictionary spelling of the following words.

roller _____

second _____

nation _____

Name: _____ Date: _____

English Warm-ups: Dictionary Skills

Name/Date: _____

DICTIONARY 7

Number the words below, putting them in alphabetical order.

_____ middle   _____ marker

_____ mean   _____ money

_____ mast   _____ mince

_____ mildew   _____ marked

Name/Date: _____

DICTIONARY 8

Add a prefix to each of the following words.

_____ hurt

_____ soak

_____ perfect

_____ agree

Name/Date: _____

DICTIONARY 9

Divide each of the following words into syllables.

mattress _____

table _____

romper _____

lucky _____

Name/Date: _____

DICTIONARY 10

Circle the words that are between these two guide words on the dictionary page.

lesson/mummy

languish   million   lump

mustard   market   link

Name/Date: _____

DICTIONARY 11

Decide if these words would come in the first third, the middle third, or the last third of a dictionary.

_____ numerical   _____ animal

_____ lemon   _____ inch

_____ pickle   _____ young

_____ violin   _____ banter

Name/Date: _____

DICTIONARY 12

Write a word that is an example of the following pronunciation symbols.

ch _____

z _____

o _____

f _____

m _____

Name: _____   Date: _____

English Warm-ups: Dictionary Skills

Name/Date: _____

DICTIONARY 13

Use a dictionary to find eight words with *im-* as a prefix.

im _____   im _____

im _____   im _____

im _____   im _____

im _____   im _____

Name/Date: _____

DICTIONARY 14

Use a dictionary to find four compound words that begin with the letter *b*. Then put them in alphabetical order.

_____   b _____

_____   b _____

_____   b _____

_____   b _____

Name/Date: _____

DICTIONARY 15

Circle the words that are be-tween these two guide words on the dictionary page.

hero/history

hesitate   handsome   hewn

high   help   harried

Name/Date: _____

DICTIONARY 16

Divide each of the following words into syl-lables.

memory _____

trustworthy _____

particularly _____

marvel _____

himself _____

Name/Date: _____

DICTIONARY 17

Use a dictionary, and look up the word *beautiful.*

How many syllables? _____

Divide it into syllables. _____

What part of speech is it? _____

Name/Date: _____

DICTIONARY 18

Number the words below, putting them in alphabetical order.

_____ wonderful   _____ dirty

_____ zebra   _____ winter

_____ every   _____ juice

_____ candy   _____ avalanche

Name: _____ Date: _____

English Warm-ups: Dictionary Skills

Name/Date: _____

DICTIONARY 19

Number the words below, putting them in alphabetical order.

_____ wander   _____ middle

_____ statue   _____ question

_____ minute   _____ curtain

_____ divide   _____ confuse

Name/Date: _____

DICTIONARY 20

For each of the following words, underline the prefix and/or suffix. Circle the base word.

runner   nondairy   unanswerable

defenseless   wonderful

Name/Date: _____

DICTIONARY 21

Write two definitions for each of these words. Write the part of speech after each definition.

produce _____

_____

wonder _____

_____

Chinese _____

_____

Name/Date: _____

DICTIONARY 22

Use a dictionary to find a synonym for each of the following words.

inflate _____

cry _____

frown _____

plain _____

Name/Date: _____

DICTIONARY 23

Divide each of the following words into syllables.

marvelous _____

phonograph _____

blanket _____

metropolis _____

bedspread _____

television _____

Name/Date: _____

DICTIONARY 24

Say each dictionary pronunciation to yourself. Write the word. Check the dictionary to see if you are correct.

těm′pər _____

păch′wûrk _____

nōz _____

dô′tər _____

21

Name: _____ Date: _____

English Warm-ups: Dictionary Skills

Name/Date: _____

DICTIONARY 25

Number the words below, putting them in alphabetical order.

_____ slippery   _____ tension

_____ defense   _____ roller

_____ seize   _____ substitute

_____ peaceful   _____ immune

Name/Date: _____

DICTIONARY 26

Write two definitions for each of these words. Write the part of speech after each definition.

American _____

_____

bolt _____

slick _____

_____

Name/Date: _____

DICTIONARY 27

Divide each of the following words into syllables.

affectionate _____

shining _____

puzzle _____

feather _____

stolen _____

Name/Date: _____

DICTIONARY 28

Use a dictionary and look up the word *remainder.*

How many syllables? _____

Divide it into syllables. _____

How many definitions? _____

Name/Date: _____

DICTIONARY 29

Say each dictionary pronunciation to yourself. Write the word. Check the dictionary to see if you are correct.

ri mo͞ov′ _____

bo͝ok _____

bi fôr′ _____

fôrth _____

with _____

Name/Date: _____

DICTIONARY 30

Circle the words that are between these two guide words on the dictionary page.

still/time

talc   stray   tackle   stoop

trick   storm   tomb

Name: _____ Date: _____

English Warm-ups: Dictionary Skills

Name/Date: _____

DICTIONARY 31

Number the words below, putting them in alphabetical order.

_____ horizontal   _____ horse

_____ hold   _____ host

_____ homing   _____ hope

_____ hobby   _____ hockey

Name/Date: _____

DICTIONARY 32

Use a dictionary to find a synonym for each of the following words.

decline _____

agitate _____

hurry _____

precise _____

vogue _____

Name/Date: _____

DICTIONARY 33

Using a dictionary, look up the following words. Write the guide words and dictionary spelling.

stretch _____

_____

connect _____

_____

special _____

_____

Name/Date: _____

DICTIONARY 34

Write the dictionary spelling for each of the following words.

never _____

cope _____

idea _____

weight _____

reign _____

Name/Date: _____

DICTIONARY 35

Circle the words that are between these two guide words on the dictionary page.

paid/quite

pain   quiet   quit   padding

pale   pail   quirk

Name/Date: _____

DICTIONARY 36

Write two definitions for each of these words. Write the part of speech after each definition.

yellow _____

_____

flower _____

_____

holiday _____

_____

Name: _____ Date: _____

English Warm-ups: Dictionary Skills

Name/Date: _____

DICTIONARY 37

Circle the words that are between these two guide words
on the dictionary page.

less/lever

letter   lasso   lettuce   let

limp   leper   lemon

Name/Date: _____

DICTIONARY 38

Write four words that begin with *photo-*.

photo _____

photo _____

photo _____

photo _____

Name/Date: _____

DICTIONARY 39

Use a dictionary to find a synonym for each
of the following words.

mistake _____

pitch _____

remain_____

moist _____

ill _____

Name/Date: _____

DICTIONARY 40

Say each dictionary pronunciation to yourself. Write the
word. Check the dictionary
to see if you are correct.

tĕl′ə fōn _____

dĕf _____

hôr′ər _____

kăch _____

Name/Date: _____

DICTIONARY 41

Number the words below, putting them in alphabetical order.

_____ dip   _____ dear

_____ dye   _____ deep

_____ donut   _____ danger

_____ driver   _____ demon

_____ dance

Name/Date: _____

DICTIONARY 42

Write a word that is an example of the following pronunciation symbols.

h _____

o͝o _____

ē _____
ĭ _____

th _____

ô _____

Name: _____ Date: _____

English Warm-ups: Dictionary Skills

Name/Date: _____

DICTIONARY 43

Write the dictionary spelling for each of the following words.

carnival _____

coat _____

ditch _____

frown _____

dollar _____

Name/Date: _____

DICTIONARY 44

Write two synonyms for each of the following words.

locate _____ _____

sulky _____ _____

final _____ _____

under _____ _____

Name/Date: _____

DICTIONARY 45

Write two definitions for the word *fair.*

_____

_____

Write two definitions for the word *lead.*

_____

_____

Name/Date: _____

DICTIONARY 46

Divide each of the following words into syllables.

classroom _____

example _____

factors _____

report _____

condition _____

elephant _____

Name/Date: _____

DICTIONARY 47

Write two definitions for each of these words. Write the part of speech after each definition.

vacation _____

_____

catch _____

_____

ticket _____

_____

Name/Date: _____

DICTIONARY 48

Use a dictionary and find a definition for each of the following words.

uniform _____

rough _____

pressed _____

catch _____

25

Name: _____ Date: _____

English Warm-ups: Spelling Skills

Name/Date: _____

SPELLING 1

Correct the spelling.

I think weave been going in circles instead of travling in a straight lign.

_____

_____

_____

_____

Name/Date: _____

SPELLING 2

Correct the sentence.

Steve maid sure that his hare was combed before going to class.

_____

_____

_____

_____

Name/Date: _____

SPELLING 3

Correct the sentence.

Who's pencil is to short to fit in the pensil sharpener?

_____

_____

_____

_____

Name/Date: _____

SPELLING 4

Correct the sentence.

Caroline is weighting for the knew movie to come to town.

_____

_____

_____

_____

Name/Date: _____

SPELLING 5

Correct the sentence.

I think the vue from the top of the hill is vary beautiful.

_____

_____

_____

_____

Name/Date: _____

SPELLING 6

Correct the sentence.

Did you by too books at the fare?

_____

_____

_____

_____

Name: _____ Date: _____

English Warm-ups: Spelling Skills

Name/Date: _____

SPELLING 7

Circle the words that are spelled incorrectly. Then write the correct spelling above the word.

underneath   spagetti   fourty

anser   because   whisper

Name/Date: _____

SPELLING 8

One spelling rule is "*i* before *e* except after *c*." Write four words that follow that rule.

_____

_____

_____

_____

Name/Date: _____

SPELLING 9

Write the plurals of the following words.

spice _____

moose _____

fantasy _____

crush _____

woman _____

house _____

fish _____

Name/Date: _____

SPELLING 10

Correct the following sentence.

Ware did you by that crazie hat?

_____

_____

_____

Name/Date: _____

SPELLING 11

Correct the following sentence.

Do you think the trane will be on tiem at the staytion?

_____

_____

_____

Name/Date: _____

SPELLING 12

Look in the dictionary for the variant spelling for each of the following words.

canceled _____

catsup _____

cantaloupe _____

labor _____

Name: _____ Date: _____

English Warm-ups: Spelling Skills

SPELLING 13

Circle the words that are spelled incorrectly. Then write the correct spelling above the word.

craul   astronaut   controlled

valleys   special   familier

geese

SPELLING 14

Write the plurals of the following words.

radio _____

roof _____

deer _____

tooth _____

shelf _____

prefix _____

hero _____

SPELLING 15

Correct the following sentence.

What are you whereing too the party tonite?

_____

_____

_____

_____

SPELLING 16

Correct the following sentence.

Did you no that sum people have never eaten spagetti and meetballs?

_____

_____

_____

SPELLING 17

Correct the following sentence.

I red a book about yung rabbits and how they live.

_____

_____

_____

SPELLING 18

Correct the following sentence.

The gooses flue South for the Winter.

_____

_____

_____

Name: _____   Date: _____

English Warm-ups: Spelling Skills

Name/Date: _____

SPELLING 19

Circle the words that are spelled incorrectly. Then write the correct spelling above the word.

physian   crying   truly

lesson   neighber   circaler

refe

Name/Date: _____

SPELLING 20

Write the plurals of the following words.

tomato _____

Saturday _____

index _____

sundae _____

studio _____

acorn _____

Name/Date: _____

SPELLING 21

Correct the following sentence.

I baught a radio-controlled car at the maul.

_____

_____

_____

_____

Name/Date: _____

SPELLING 22

Add prefixes and suffixes to these roots to make words. See how many words you can make.

port   spect   aud   tract

_____

_____

_____

Name/Date: _____

SPELLING 23

Correct the following sentence.

There are too vallies in our town.

_____

_____

_____

_____

Name/Date: _____

SPELLING 24

Correct the following sentence.

The astronaught tested the space vehecle in the dessert.

_____

_____

_____

Name: _____ Date: _____

English Warm-ups: Spelling Skills

Name/Date: _____

SPELLING 25

Make a list of antonyms for the word *cold*.

_____   _____

_____   _____

_____   _____

_____   _____

_____   _____

Name/Date: _____

SPELLING 26

Sometimes we double the final consonant when adding an ending. Make a list of words that double the final consonant and a list of those that don't.

_____   _____

_____   _____

_____   _____

_____   _____

Name/Date: _____

SPELLING 27

Make a list of words that have *eco* as the root.

_____   _____

_____   _____

_____   _____

_____   _____

_____   _____

Name/Date: _____

SPELLING 28

Correct the following sentence.

Aisle go to the store for you if you will weight a minite.

_____

_____

_____

Name/Date: _____

SPELLING 29

Circle the words that are spelled incorrectly. Then write the correct spelling above the word.

diffrent   yeild   expect   receive

alirt   monkeys   columm

Name/Date: _____

SPELLING 30

Make a list of words that have *-tion* as an ending, and then make a list of words that have *-sion* as an ending.

_____   _____

_____   _____

_____   _____

_____   _____

_____   _____

Name: _____ Date: _____

English Warm-ups: Spelling Skills

Name/Date: _____

SPELLING 31

Circle the words that are spelled incorrectly. Then write the correct spelling above the word.

assinement   experimental

florol   approvel

tolarate   receipt

Name/Date: _____

SPELLING 32

Make a list of words that have the *-able* suffix. Do you always drop the *e* before adding the suffix? Give some examples of each.

_____ _____
_____ _____
_____ _____
_____ _____
_____ _____

Name/Date: _____

SPELLING 33

Look in the dictionary for the variant spelling for each of the following words.

travelog _____

busses _____

grey _____

likeable _____

Name/Date: _____

SPELLING 34

Correct the following sentence.

Are computer mounitor has a wavie line that goes threw the center of the screan.

_____
_____
_____

Name/Date: _____

SPELLING 35

Make a list of synonyms for the word *sleep*.

_____ _____
_____ _____
_____ _____
_____ _____

Name/Date: _____

SPELLING 36

Write five words that can be used as a noun or a verb.

_____
_____
_____
_____
_____

Name: _____ Date: _____

English Warm-ups: Spelling Skills

Name/Date: _____

SPELLING 37

Correct the following sentence.

The North wind blue thru the old windows of the hawse.

_____

_____

_____

Name/Date: _____

SPELLING 38

Run is a noun and a verb. Write five other words that can be nouns **and** verbs.

_____

_____

_____

_____

_____

Name/Date: _____

SPELLING 39

Write six words that have the prefix *anti-*.

anti _____

anti _____

anti _____

anti _____

anti _____

anti _____

Name/Date: _____

SPELLING 40

Circle the words that are spelled incorrectly. Then write the correct spelling above the word.

nuculer   elamentry

unnecessary   unusal

beged   electritian

Name/Date: _____

SPELLING 41

Correct the following sentence.

Mom asked michael to git his feat off the furnature.

_____

_____

_____

Name/Date: _____

SPELLING 42

Think of three compound words that go with *drop*.

_____

_____

_____

Name: _____   Date: _____

English Warm-ups: Spelling Skills

Name/Date: _____

SPELLING 43

Correct the following sentence.

Wood you beleive that onece people thought the world was flat?

_____

_____

_____

Name/Date: _____

SPELLING 44

Correct the following sentence.

Coud you git me a glasse of water and a sandwitch?

_____

_____

_____

Name/Date: _____

SPELLING 45

Write six words that have the suffix -ness.

_____ **ness**

_____ **ness**

_____ **ness**

_____ **ness**

_____ **ness**

_____ **ness**

Name/Date: _____

SPELLING 46

Circle the words that are spelled incorrectly. Then write the correct spelling above the word.

scrach   happened

meant   timming

beleif   happyness

Name/Date: _____

SPELLING 47

Correct the following sentence.

Please lie the books on the tabel with the red clothe on it.

_____

_____

_____

Name/Date: _____

SPELLING 48

Write six words that have the prefix de-.

de _____

de _____

de _____

de _____

de _____

de _____

Name: _____ Date: _____

English Warm-ups: Reading Skills

Name/Date: _____

READING 1

Circle the words that do not belong.

apple   banana   bean

pear   peas   grape

potato   orange

Why don't they belong?

_____

Name/Date: _____

READING 2

Complete the analogy.

Hot is to cold as summer is to

_____.

Name/Date: _____

READING 3

Read each sentence. Then circle the facts and underline the opinions.

Dogs make the best pets.

An Airedale is a dog.

Dogs can be trained to do tricks.

Big dogs are mean.

Name/Date: _____

READING 4

Number the following steps in order.

_____ Put the pieces of bread together.

_____ Spread the peanut butter on one slice of bread.

_____ Get out bread, peanut butter, and jelly.

_____ Spread jelly on one slice of bread.

_____ Cut the sandwich in half.

Name/Date: _____

READING 5

Circle the words that rhyme.

stare   star   hair

stair   hare   start

Name/Date: _____

READING 6

Write a title for the paragraph below.

_____

   Picnics are one of the the best ways to eat dinner during the summer. You can take sandwiches or chicken, potato salad, and brownies in a basket and go to the park to eat. After dinner, you can play a game or catch fireflies when it gets dark.

Name: _____ Date: _____

English Warm-ups: Reading Skills

READING 7

Complete the following analogies.

Fish is to pond as bird is to

_____.

Caterpillar is to cocoon as turtle is to

_____.

READING 8

Read each sentence. Then circle the facts and underline the opinions.

Horses are fun to ride.

Horses were used in the West on ranches to herd cattle.

I think horses are beautiful animals.

Most horses can be trained to do tricks.

READING 9

Read the following words. Circle the ones that rhyme.

night   write   weight

slight   site   blight

READING 10

Number the following steps in order.

_____ Put the chocolate sauce on the scoop of ice cream.

_____ Take the ice cream out of the freezer.

_____ Scoop the ice cream out of the container.

_____ Get a bowl to put the ice cream in.

READING 11

What is the theme of a story with these words?

sleds   snow   hill

bonfire   tree

_____

_____

READING 12

Read each sentence. Then circle the cause, and underline the effect.

Carol took two books with her because the car ride would be several hours long.

Since the gate was open, the dog ran away.

Name: _____ Date: _____

English Warm-ups: Reading Skills

READING 13

What is the theme of a story with these words?

tennis   racquet   serve

fall   scrape

_____

READING 14

Read each sentence. Then circle the facts and underline the opinions.

Fish live in water.

The fish at the aquarium are beautiful.

Fish make the best pets.

Fish breathe through gills.

READING 15

Complete the following analogies.

Fur is to bear as scales are to

_____.

Arm is to human as _____

is to bird.

READING 16

Read each sentence. Then circle the cause and underline the effect.

Tom fell off his bike when it hit a pothole.

We will get free time if the class finishes this

assignment.

READING 17

Read the following paragraph. Then describe the character on your own paper.

    He sat in his wheelchair, his grey hair neatly combed. Mr. White shivered in the chilly wind. The children waved as they went by on their way home from school, and he smiled and said hello.

READING 18

Number the following steps in order.

_____ Spread the jelly on the toast.

_____ Put the bread in the toaster.

_____ Spread the butter on the toast.

_____ Turn on the toaster.

_____ Get the bread out of the bag.

Name: _____ Date: _____

English Warm-ups: Reading Skills

Name/Date: _____

READING 19

Complete the following analogies.

Panel is to door as pane is to

_____.

Eye is to vision as ear is to

_____.

Name/Date: _____

READING 20

Circle the cause and underline the effect.

The egg rolled off the counter when the cat pushed it.

Because the ice was rough, the skater fell down.

Name/Date: _____

READING 21

Circle the word that does not belong.

eyes   nose   chin

ears   mouth

Why doesn't it belong?

_____

Name/Date: _____

READING 22

Circle the word that does not belong.

level   race car   dog

peep   eye

Why doesn't it belong?

_____

Name/Date: _____

READING 23

What is the main idea of this list of words?

leaves, rake, brisk wind, warm jacket

_____

_____

Name/Date: _____

READING 24

Think of two effects for this cause.

Because the wind blew the door open ...

_____

_____

_____

37

Name: _____ Date: _____

English Warm-ups: Reading Skills

READING 25

What do you think will happen next in this story?

   The sled was heading down the hill, picking up speed every foot of the way. Jamie tried to steer, but the sled seemed to have a mind of its own. He could see the tree ahead.

_____

_____

READING 26

Circle the word that does not belong.

scroll ball   joystick   keyboard

mouse   printer

Why doesn't it belong?

_____

READING 27

What might Jennifer be doing?

Jennifer got a bowl, flour, and chocolate chips from the cupboard.

_____

_____

_____

READING 28

Complete the following analogies.

Bed is to bedroom as desk is to

_____.

Legs are to table as wheels are to

_____.

READING 29

Circle the word that does not belong.

chicken   rabbit   dog

cat   horse

Why doesn't it belong?

_____

READING 30

Read the following sentences. Circle the facts, and underline the opinions.

New York is a beautiful city.

The Empire State Building is in New York.

The best restaurants are in New York.

Immigrants came through Ellis Island and then went to New York.

Name: _____ Date: _____

English Warm-ups: Reading Skills

Name/Date: _____

READING 31

The breeze gently blew through the window. Ming rushed down the stairs to join her family for breakfast. Wow, no school for a whole three months!

What time of day is it?

_____

What season of the year?

_____

Name/Date: _____

READING 32

LaKeisha erased her writing. "Dad, what is a six-letter word for travel?" she asked.

What is LaKeisha doing?

_____

_____

_____

Name/Date: _____

READING 33

Write two sentences using personification.

_____

_____

_____

_____

_____

Name/Date: _____

READING 34

Read the following sentences. Circle the facts and underline the opinions.

The baseball team played a terrible game. The pitcher only struck out two people. The first baseman didn't catch the throw from third base. They should let Juan play.

Name/Date: _____

READING 35

Circle the word that does not belong.

write   butter   fold

cut   tear

Why doesn't it belong?

_____

Name/Date: _____

READING 36

Read the following sentence. Then circle the cause, and underline the effect.

The roar of the cars made it difficult for the fans to hear the announcer.

Name: _____ Date: _____

English Warm-ups: Reading Skills

Name/Date: _____

READING 37

Read the following sentence. Then circle the cause and underline the effect.

When the power went out, Mom lit some

candles.

Name/Date: _____

READING 38

Write the title of an article to inform.

_____

Write the title of an article to persuade.

_____

Name/Date: _____

READING 39

Write a metaphor.

_____

_____

_____

_____

Name/Date: _____

READING 40

Mrs. Jones was slicing an apple. "Ow!" she cried.

What happened to Mrs. Jones?

_____

_____

_____

Name/Date: _____

READING 41

Complete the following analogies.

Monitor is to computer as

_____ is to book.

Pencil is to paper as

_____ is to computer.

Name/Date: _____

READING 42

Matt answered the phone. He went running down the stairs and yelled at the top of his lungs, "Mom, you'll never guess, I ..."

What did Matt tell his mom?

_____

_____

Name: _____   Date: _____

English Warm-ups: Reading Skills

READING 43

Write a simile.

_____

_____

_____

_____

READING 44

What is the theme of a story containing these words?

palm tree   suntan lotion   ocean

sand   swimming suit

_____

READING 45

Annie tested the microphone. Then she straightened her shoulders and looked out over the audience.

What is Annie about to do?

_____

_____

_____

READING 46

Write an effect for this cause.

The ball was hit right toward Mr. Evans' house.

_____

_____

_____

READING 47

Li bundled up against the wind. He walked to the school playground. He saw wreaths on doors, decorations on a classroom's windows, and carols could be heard coming from a house nearby.

What season of the year is it?

_____

What holiday is it? _____

READING 48

Write a cause for this effect.

Jelly beans spilled all over the floor.

_____

_____

_____

Answer Keys

Story Leads 1–48
Answers will vary.

Grammar/Usage 3 (p. 10)
children   oxen   mice

Grammar/Usage 4 (p. 10)
Subject: Jeff   Verb: carried
Subject: fish   Verb: are

Grammar/Usage 5 (p. 10)
I was late for school, but I wasn't marked tardy.

Grammar/Usage 7 (p. 11)
Babe Ruth held the home run record for many years; it was broken by Hank Aaron.

Grammar/Usage 8 (p. 11)
They made their playhouse out of boxes their mother gave them.

Grammar/Usage 11 (p. 11)
men's   sisters'   pennies'   bananas'

Grammar/Usage 14 (p. 12)
Puppies are born with their eyes closed, and they stay near the mother dog.

Grammar/Usage 17 (p. 12)
I would like to take Spanish next year.

Grammar/Usage 19 (p. 13)
Our science teacher, Mr. Langenbach, shows us how to do experiments.

Grammar/Usage 20 (p. 13)
well
good

Grammar/Usage 22 (p. 13)
Answers will vary. Possible answers include:
would've   I'll   could've   I'm

Grammar/Usage 23 (p. 13)
Did you know some birds can't fly?

Grammar/Usage 25 (p. 14)
Answers will vary. Possible answers include:
shrimp   fish   deer   sheep

Grammar/Usage 26 (p. 14)
A full-grown hummingbird weighs only a few ounces.

Grammar/Usage 28 (p. 14)
Answers will vary. Possible answers include:
rather   quite   very   never

Grammar/Usage 29 (p. 14)
Using its paws, the cat knocked the ball across the floor.

Grammar/Usage 32 (p. 15)
I   we   you   they   he   she   it
Sentences will vary.

Grammar/Usage 34 (p. 15)
Don't stack the books too high; they will fall over and hurt someone.

Grammar/Usage 35 (p. 15)
First put on socks, and then put on shoes.

Grammar/Usage 36 (p. 15)
Answers will vary. Possible answers include:
scissors   jeans   pants   trousers

Grammar/Usage 37 (p. 16)
You are going to the movies.
Jason did eat the cake.
Many books are on the table.

Grammar/Usage 38 (p. 16)
Woodrow Wilson began the League of Nations, but the United States never joined.

Grammar/Usage 40 (p. 16)
swim: swam, swum   play: played, played
run: ran, run

Grammar/Usage 41 (p. 16)
Answers will vary. Possible answers include:
warm: cool   quick: slow
forget: remember   fiction: nonfiction
shiny: dull   midnight: noon

Grammar/Usage 42 (p. 16)
Yes, I think the answer to question one should be Mr. Washington.

Grammar/Usage 44 (p. 17)
The explorers who had traveled to Mexico brought back gold and silver to their country.

Grammar/Usage 45 (p. 17)
Answers will vary. Possible answers include:
leaf - leaves   hoof - hooves
half - halves   thief - thieves

Grammar/Usage 46 (p. 17)
Mister: Mr.   doctor: dr.
street: st.   January: Jan.
Professor: Prof.   hour: hr.
quart: qt.   avenue: ave.

Grammar/Usage 47 (p. 17)
Subject: Stephen   Verb: ran
Subject: Stephanie   Verb: is

Dictionary 1 (p. 18)
4 enzyme   1 balloon
5 special   3 doughnut
2 carpet   6 triple

Dictionary 2 (p. 18)
pecan   spat   beach

Dictionary 3 (p. 18)
un · u · su · al   dis · tance   im · por · tant

Dictionary 4 (p. 18)
grasp   grape   graph

Dictionary 5 (p. 18)
baker   bask

Dictionary 6 (p. 18)
rō′ lər   sek′ ənd   nā′ shən

Dictionary 7 (p. 19)
5 middle   2 marker
4 mean   8 money
3 mast   7 mince
6 mildew   1 marked

Dictionary 8 (p. 19)
Answers will vary. Possible answers include:
unhurt   presoak   imperfect   disagree

Dictionary 9 (p. 20)
mat · tress   ta · ble   romp · er   luck · y

Dictionary 10 (p. 19)
million   lump   market   link

Dictionary 11 (p. 19)
numerical: middle   animal: first
lemon: middle   inch: middle
pickle: middle   young: last
violin: last   banter: first

Dictionary 12 (p. 19)
Answers will vary. Possible answers include:
church   zebra   pop   fence   man

Dictionary 15 (p. 20)
hesitate   hewn   high

Dictionary 16 (p. 20)
mem · o · ry   trust · wor · thy   par · tic · u · lar · ly
mar · vel   him · self

Dictionary 17 (p. 20)
three syllables
beau · ti · ful
adjective

Dictionary 18 (p. 20)
7 wonderful   3 dirty
8 zebra   6 winter
4 every   5 juice
2 candy   1 avalanche

Dictionary 19 (p. 21)
8 wander   4 middle
7 statue   6 question
5 minute   2 curtain
3 divide   1 confuse

Dictionary 20 (p. 21)
runner   nondairy   unanswerable
defenseless   wonderful

Dictionary 21 (p. 21)
produce: noun/verb   wonder: noun/verb
Chinese: noun/adjective

Dictionary 22 (p. 21)
Answers will vary. Possible answers include:
inflate: swell   cry: weep
frown: grimace   plain: unadorned

Dictionary 23 (p. 21)
mar · vel · ous   pho · no · graph   blan · ket
me · trop · o · lis   bed · spread   tel · e · vi · sion

Dictionary 24 (p. 21)
temper   patchwork   nose   daughter

Dictionary 25 (p. 22)
6 slippery   8 tension
1 defense   4 roller
5 seize   7 substitute
3 peaceful   2 immune

Dictionary 26 (p. 22)
American: adjective/noun   bolt: noun/verb
slick: adjective/verb/noun

Dictionary 27 (p. 22)
af · fec · tion · ate   shin · ing   puz · zle
feath · er   sto · len

Dictionary 28 (p. 22)
three syllables
re · main · der
three definitions

Dictionary 29 (p. 22)
remove   book   before   forth/fourth   with

Dictionary 30 (p. 22)
talc   stray   tackle   stoop   storm

Dictionary 31 (p. 23)
6 horizontal   7 horse
3 hold   8 host
4 homing   5 hope
1 hobby   2 hockey

Dictionary 32 (p. 23)
Answers will vary. Possible answers include:
decline: refuse   agitate: stir   hurry: rush
precise: exact   vogue: style

Dictionary 33 (p. 23)
Guide words will vary.
strech   kə nekt′   spesh′ əl

Dictionary 34 (p. 23)
nev′ ər   kōp   ī dē′ ə
wāt   rān

Dictionary 35 (p. 23)
pain   quiet   quit   pale   pail   quirk

Dictionary 36 (p. 23)
yellow: adjective/verb   flower: noun/verb
holiday: noun/adjective

Dictionary 37 (p. 24)
letter   lettuce   let

Dictionary 39 (p. 24)
Answers will vary. Possible answers include:
mistake: error   pitch: throw   remain: stay
moist: damp   ill: sick

Dictionary 40 (p. 24)
telephone   deaf   horror   catch

Dictionary 41 (p. 24)
6 dip   3 dear
9 dye   4 deep
7 donut   2 danger
8 driver   5 demon
1 dance

Dictionary 42 (p. 24)
Answers will vary. Possible answers include:
hold   look   feet   sick   father   forty

Dictionary 43 (p. 25)
kär′ nə vəl   kōt   dich
froun   däl′ ər

Dictionary 44 (p. 25)
Answers will vary. Possible answers include:
locate: find, spot   sulky: sad, pouty
final: end, concluding   under: beneath, below

Dictionary 45 (p. 25)
Answers will vary. Possible answers include:
fair: just; attractive; light; a carnival or festival
lead: to guide or direct; a heavy metal element

Dictionary 46 (p. 25)
class · room   ex · am · ple   fac · tors
re · port   con · di · tion   el · e · phant

Dictionary 47 (p. 25)
vacation: noun/verb/adjective   catch: noun/verb
ticket: noun/verb/adjective

Spelling 1 (p. 26)
I think we've been going in circles instead of traveling in
a straight line.

Spelling 2 (p. 26)
Steve made sure that his hair was combed before going
to class.

Spelling 3 (p. 26)
Whose pencil is too short to fit in the pencil sharpener?

Spelling 4 (p. 26)
Caroline is waiting for the new movie to come to town.

Spelling 5 (p. 26)
I think the view from the top of the hill is very beautiful.

Spelling 6 (p. 26)
Did you buy two books at the fair?

Spelling 7 (p. 27)
spaghetti   forty   answer

Spelling 8 (p. 27)
Answers will vary. Possible answers include:
receive   perceive   sieve   pier

Spelling 9 (p. 27)
spices   moose   fantasies   crushes   women
houses   fish/fishes

Spelling 10 (p. 27)
Where did you buy that crazy hat?

Spelling 11 (p. 27)
Do you think the train will be on time at the station?

Spelling 12 (p. 27)
cancelled   ketchup   cantaloup   labour

Spelling 13 (p. 28)
crawl   familiar

Spelling 14 (p. 28)
radios   roofs   deer   teeth   shelves   prefixes
heroes

Spelling 15 (p. 28)
What are you wearing to the party tonight?

Spelling 16 (p. 28)
Did you know that some people have never eaten spaghetti and meatballs?

Spelling 17 (p. 28)
I read a book about young rabbits and how they live.

Spelling 18 (p. 28)
The geese flew south for the winter.

Spelling 19 (p. 29)
physician   neighbor   circular   reef

Spelling 20 (p. 29)
tomatoes   Saturdays   indexes   sundaes   studios
acorns

Spelling 21 (p. 29)
I bought a radio-controlled car at the mall.

Spelling 23 (p. 29)
There are two valleys in our town.

Spelling 24 (p. 29)
The astronaut tested the space vehicle in the desert.

Spelling 28 (p. 30)
I'll go to the store for you if you will wait a minute.

Spelling 29 (p. 30)
different   yield   alert   column

Spelling 31 (p. 31)
assignment   floral   approval   tolerate

Spelling 33 (p. 31)
travelogue   buses   gray   likable

Spelling 34 (p. 31)
Our computer monitor has a wavy line that goes through the center of the screen.

Spelling 37 (p. 32)
The north wind blew through the old windows of the house.

Spelling 40 (p. 32)
nuclear   elementary   unusual   begged   electrician

Spelling 41 (p. 32)
Mom asked Michael to get his feet off the furniture.

Spelling 43 (p. 33)
Would you believe that once people thought the world was flat?

Spelling 44 (p. 33)
Could you get me a glass of water and a sandwich?

Spelling 46 (p. 33)
scratch   timing   belief   happiness

Spelling 47 (p. 33)
Please lay the books on the table with the red cloth on it.

Reading 1 (p. 34)
bean   peas   potato
They are vegetables, not fruits.

Reading 2 (p. 34)
winter

Reading 3 (p. 34)
Facts: An Airedale is a dog.
          Dogs can be trained to do tricks.

Reading 4 (p. 34)
4, 2, 1, 3, 5 or 4, 3, 1, 2, 5

Reading 5 (p. 34)
stare   hair   stair   hare

Reading 7 (p. 35)
nest   egg

Reading 8 (p. 35)
Facts: Horses were used in the West on ranches to
         herd cattle.
         Most horses can be trained to do tricks.

Reading 9 (p. 35)
night   write   slight   site   blight

Reading 10 (p. 35)
4, 2, 3, 1

Reading 12 (p. 35)
Cause: because the car ride would be several hours
long.
Effect: Carol took two books with her
Cause: Since the gate was open,
Effect: the dog ran away.

Reading 14 (p. 36)
Facts: Fish live in water.
         Fish breathe through gills.

Reading 15 (p. 36)
fish   wing

Reading 16 (p. 36)
Cause: it hit a pothole.
Effect: Tom fell off his bike
Cause: the class finishes this assignment.
Effect: We will get free time

Reading 17 (p. 36)
Possible answers: old, distinguished, disabled, friendly

Reading 18 (p. 36)
5, 2, 4, 3, 1

Reading 19 (p. 37)
window   hearing

Reading 20 (p. 37)
Cause: the cat pushed it.
Effect: The egg rolled off the counter
Cause: Because the ice was rough
Effect: the skater fell down.

Reading 21 (p. 37)
ears: Not on front of face. OR
chin: Not a sensing organ.

Reading 22 (p. 37)
dog: It is not a palindrome.

Reading 26 (p. 38)
printer: It is not an input device.

Reading 28 (p. 38)
office/classroom   car/truck

Reading 29 (p. 38)
chicken: It doesn't have four legs, isn't a mammal, and
doesn't have fur.

Reading 30 (p. 38)
Facts: The Empire State Building is in New York.
         Immigrants came through Ellis Island and then
         went to New York.

Reading 31 (p. 39)
morning   summer

Reading 32 (p. 39)
a crossword puzzle

Reading 34 (p. 39)
Facts: The pitcher only struck out two people.
         The first baseman didn't catch the throw from
         third base.

Reading 35 (p. 39)
butter: It does not have to do with paper.

Reading 36 (p. 39)
Cause: The roar of the cars
Effect: made it difficult for the fans to hear the announcer.

Reading 37 (p. 40)
Cause: When the power went out,
Effect: Mom lit some candles.

Reading 41 (p. 40)
page   mouse/keyboard

Reading 47 (p. 41)
winter   Christmas